T0195025

THE BOOK of NOREMAC

CAN YOU HELP NOREMAC FIND HIMSELF?

Cameron Pendleton
& Jaden Townes

BALBOA.PRESS
A DIVISION OF HAY HOUSE

Balboa Press books may be ordered through booksellers or by contacting:

Balboa Press
A Division of Hay House
1663 Liberty Drive
Bloomington, IN 47403
www.balboapress.com
1 (877) 407-4847

Print information available on the last page.

ISBN: 978-1-9822-3857-5 (sc)
ISBN: 978-1-9822-3858-2 (e)

Balboa Press rev. date: 11/12/2019

Contentment

To find true happiness, you must find peace within oneself, but growing up around this generation of people true happiness doesn't seem to exist. Hi, my name is Noremac I am 18 years old, my father abandoned me when I was 7 years old, but from him not being here physically he still motivated me to become a better man he would never get a chance to be. People wonder how he motivated me when he wasn't really in my life, I guess I just turned negative energy into positive energy and forgave him for his mistakes, but I shall never forget what he had done to me. My mother on the other hand is the reason why I am who I am today. A strong, Intelligent, young man sort of like a majority of my generation male population, but we as teenagers fail to acknowledge the good in education. "People Acknowledge Knowledge Only If Their Mind Consist of Knowledge" ... a quote by a wise one which resembles anyone who is not openminded. Life will bring so much pain, hatred, and desires but nothing can compare to a piece of mind. The mind is what makes this world different because everyone thinks and processes information differently. Even though you are considered weird or abnormal by not thinking like the person in front of you, you must learn to love yourself that is the only way to find true bliss. I can only find true bliss by staying to myself and writing about how I'm feeling at that moment. I rather write notes to myself then to tell my secrets to a listening ear which later turns into a running mouth. I was forced to grow up early due to my father mistakes, His actions impacted my adolescent years because it forced me to change my mindset towards life. I must work on becoming a man, wondering what I should do after high school, instead of just being a kid living life in the moment like everyone else, But I don't consider myself living I'm more so existing. I question my neurons every night before bed asking them how to be a father? how to be a man? how to teach my son to be a man? how to teach my daughter to focus on her career & not these stupid boys? how to be something I was never taught to be? Then and There I knew my journey will be longer than I expected on the search to find Noremac.

Contents

1

Viewpoint

Growing up there were several groups and clicks you could easily be a part of without giving your consent. The nerds, the most hated group in high school, all the girls wanted the boys who skip class & get into trouble, but always sleep on the ones with 4.0 GPA's, goals, & point of views. The introverts, ones who speak only when spoken to, their circles are microscopic, & they are very standoffish when it comes to strangers. The dissimilar group or shall I say the abnormal group, I chose to be affiliated with this group because everyone in this group are unique when it comes to how they live their day to day lives. I also tried being a bad boy, introvert, a smart bad boy, & just a normal teenager, but I couldn't seem to fit in any other group. This group understood me as a person & they liked me for me.

I always loved walking in the shoes of other people to see what their life is like at home, maybe I can figure out the reason why they act the way they do in school & around certain people. The members of the dissimilar group are Nedaj, Nomad, Novad, & now me Noremac.

Nedaj the oldest member of the group he is one creative fella when it comes to music & the subliminal messages behind it. Then we have Nomad, the creative pothead he is great at acting out scenes of movies & having you think something is wrong when it's really not. Lastly, Novad the brawler of the group, he is always prepared to fight regardless if it's physically or mentally. September 5th, 2018 the first day of 12th grade year, me and the crew were headed to class when we overheard a conversation between these two sophomore girls, they were teasing a freshman because her uniform had holes in them & they were filthy like she rolled around in mud before school started. The freshman began to cry after processing all the negative words that was being said to her by the sophomore's & she charged to the bathroom filled with anger & sorrow. "Hey!! what's your problem"? Nedaj said to the sophomore girls "mind your business" said the two sophomore's walking away laughing. "These kids are crazy already bro & classes didn't even start yet, but I will catch you guys later" Nedaj said. When the crew went to class, I waited for the anonymous girl to leave the bathroom, to kill time I started thinking to myself should I be like the bully? should I be the innocent victim of the situation?

Or should I somehow place myself in both of their shoes to see both sides of the story.

After waiting for 10 minutes the bathroom door screeched open, I stood up to greet the unknown girl. Hello, my name is Noremac, what's your name? "Octavia" the unknown girl said in a low soft tone. Are you okay? Why were those girls teasing you? "They were teasing me because I have huge holes in my uniform," Octavia said. Don't pay those girls any attention just continue to wear your clothes the way you want."The reason why I look this way is because I'm homeless & my mother didn't have any money to buy me a fresh uniform", Octavia said. Here take my uniform I have an extra one in my backpack, "are you sure"? Octavia said. Yes, I'm sure you need it more than I do. "Thank you so much god bless you", Octavia said. My pleasure. As I walked away from Octavia, I wondered what life is like being homeless, so I thought about doing a little home experiment. After school let out, I went home & took a nice long nap, as I laid under the covers it felt like my body was trapped inside of a cocoon, but I had enough room to allow my head to breathe. I started to paint pictures in my mind constantly repeating to myself what if I was homeless? & after saying it for the tenth time, I was now living in the mind of a homeless individual.

I opened my eyes slowly & I seen a man laying across from me on a flat box he had holes all in his clothes too just like Octavia. I started looking around where I was laying, & I was in a busted-up tent with dirty smelly clothes on with a bowl of change in between my legs. Where am I? I said to myself, "you are under the Polk Ville Bridge" a mysterious man said. Who are you? I said, "I am Hamilton... George Hamilton nice to meet you young man". I hesitated to shake his hand, I didn't know if he was being friendly or was he just trying to cross contaminate whatever he has in his hand over to me. Hello, I'm Noremac, but how did I end up here? "Well son your living inside of your thoughts, aren't you the kid that wished to be homeless"? Yes, that was me I said. "Come on boy let me give you a tour of your new home" George said while chuckling. "Here is where you will sleep while you are here for the time being," It was an old flattened meat box from the supermarket. "This is the sign you will use to get other folks attention, the sign says, "Hungry & Tired but Will Work for Money" No! No! I can't do this. "What do you mean son" George said, my stomach is rumbling from lack of meals, my clothes are old & stinky, I'm living off the change from people ash trays, I can't take it anymore WAKE UP, WAKE UP, WAKE UP!!!!!

Screaming from the top of my lungs, my eyes opened & I was back into reality with fresh spotless clothes on, & no bowl of change in between my legs. Wow that was a horrible dream, now I understand how Octavia feels whenever someone in school bullies her. The next morning at school I talked with the crew about what I just recently experienced they all thought it was wicked because I went from thinking about being homeless to dreaming about it. After I made the decision not to fill the shoes of anybody who is homeless, now I wanted to walk in someone else's shoes, but I just didn't know who. While class was in session, I wanted to go in the hall to observe & to scope the place out, but my teacher always caught me when I tried to sneak out the classroom. Ms. Johnson may I use the restroom? "Yes, you may but I will be watching you" Ms. Johnson said. As I walked out the room, she stood at the door to make sure I was really going to the bathroom. When I walked into the bathroom, I heard a kid sniffling like he had a load of boogers in his nose. I slowly approached the stall & it was a kid sitting on the toilet penetrating his arm with a syringe & snorting a white substance off a loose sheet of paper. Dude what the hell are you doing? "Don't tell anyone I did this, or you will regret it", the unknown kid said. I ignored his words & left the bathroom confused & lost for words.

2

Stupefacient

Yesterday I spotted a teen abusing drugs in the boys bathroom on the 3rd floor, my intentions were to knock the substance out of his hand & say "Don't Do Drugs" but that would only start a long-term conflict. I wanted to learn more about drugs & whether or not should I follow in the unknown kid footsteps. I wanted to try the drug he was using, I wanted to feel how he felt when he shot the substance into his veins, maybe it could help me cope with upcoming stress. The perfect person I could talk to about this situation is Nomad. He sits in his room for hours & just take notes on different types of drugs & how the human body responds to the drug. Let me give Nomad a call real quick. Ring!! Ring!! Ring!! "Hello" Yo Nomad? "Yeah what's up bro"? Nomad said, I have a question about this narcotic. Long story short I seen a kid in the bathroom shooting drugs into his veins & sniffing a white substance off a sheet of paper. But inside the syringe was some type of liquid. Can you help me figure out what it was? "Sure, bro just give me 24 hours & I will have the information for you", Nomad said. The next day in school Nomad gave me the information about the narcotics, the name of the drugs are "Heroin" & "Cocaine", but many people call them "Blow", "Boy", "Base", & many other weird names. "Yo Noremac these drugs are nothing to play with, you have two types of side effects which are short term & long term.

Short term effects of Heroin are nausea, vomiting, pain in the upper abdomen, & severe itching. Long term affects of Cocaine include permanent damage to blood vessels of heart and brain, tactile hallucinations, weight loss, destruction of tissues in nose if sniffed & etc. See these drugs are vicious & I don't want you getting near it bro", Nomad said. I just wanted to see what the hype was all about & whether I should try it or not. "Don't do that stuff homie I'm serious" Nomad said. Later that day I came across the kid that I saw shooting the drugs into his arm & I interrogated him. Hey!! I saw you shooting heroin in your arm yesterday how did it make you feel? "Dude what is your problem", the drug addict said. Were you sleepy afterwards? Was this a one-time thing? Or are you truly an addict? "Leave me alone you freak", the drug addict said. I watched him sprint down the hallway in terror, but from the looks of it he is ashamed to speak on his addiction. After school I went home & did a little research myself & gathered some additional information on Cocaine & Heroin. Cocaine fascinated me more than heroin & I don't know why. I found out that Cocaine is an ingredient in Coca Cola soda, but the world doesn't know about it. Technically I'm an addict now because Coca Cola is my favorite soda. Should I stop drinking them? My body is telling me continue, but my thoughts is telling me no, who do I listen to? Forget it I have to have me a nice cold Coke even if I do become an addict.

Wait a second am I losing my mind? Am I becoming an addict? Holy crap!! I'm an addict!!! "Noremac are you okay honey" my mother said. Yes, mom just screaming at the tv as usual, "Okay well dinner is in the microwave whenever you get hungry okay"? Okay thanks mom, now that she's gone, I can go back to being insane. Later that day I found out the boy in the bathroom was suffering from depression, so he started using Cocaine & Heroin because they were the only drugs that could help him cope with his pain. I would never use a substance to cope with my pain I would be a man & deal with it even though sometimes the stress can become overwhelming, but it all depends on how bad the stress is. Well what do you know? I said to myself in the mirror, who knows how I may feel 5 years from now. I may break & start using narcotics to cope you will never know until you get to that point in life. I may even become an addict because once you try it there's a 50% chance you will try it again & enjoy it even more. People fail to realize that once your temporary high is over the pain, stress & other problems comes right back. I just don't get it maybe that's why I'm alone because I don't do any type of narcotics. I bet if I did, I would have all the girls you could think of. Too bad this generation of kids fail to acknowledge the good in someone, but from a mile away can spot a spliff.

Of course, the kid that was doing drugs in the bathroom stall Is a bad boy. He already has a couple girls wrapped around his fingers while I'm just sitting here looking like an empty grocery store bag just flying in the winds. I'm worthless compared to these other kids around here, maybe I should start smoking spliffs, so I can get a taste of popularity. I guess now I need a coping mechanism now because I'm just sitting here looking at my reflection in the mirror drowning in my own thoughts just thinking about things I would never mention to my friends. Maybe I should go to sleep & allow my mind to dream about all the things I wish to have in life. I just can't seem to find myself no matter how hard I try. I started screaming "Thanks a lot sperm donor for giving me the opportunity to breathe the same air as you, now come out of the shadows & be a father. It's like when I think about one problem it triggers another one, maybe because I tend to hold a lot of pain inside instead of talking to people letting the stress flow freely, but at the end of the day I'm only hurting myself. After stressing myself out in the mirror, I started to think about this girl that I seen at school. Her name is Leugram she was so beautiful, her brown eyes were bright as the sun, her skin was smooth as a baby's bottom, she walks like she belongs on the world's next top model, but for now the hallways is her runway. I just wish one day I will have the guts to approach her.

3

False Endearment

In high school I could never seem to find the right girl because they always looked for potential & intelligence in bullies & bad boys. Teens like me were laughed at & stepped on by others. But the girl Leuqram she was a good friend to me, but there were days when she made me feel special & days when she ignores me for no apparent reason. At the same time, I thought to myself maybe I wasn't good enough for her. I was smart, with no job, no social life, & I came home every day afterschool to study. Nobody wanted a guy like me, I have dreams & goals, but me & Leu seen life from different point of views. I'm such an overthinker so over time I begin to assume things that may or may not be true. Rumors were going around the school saying Leu had a crush on me, but I couldn't believe it just didn't seem real to me. Why me out of all the guys at school? But I was too late she started dating someone, my mind became distorted & I was highly confused. I guess I wasn't good enough, all I wanted was to love & cherish her, to fill her heart with joy & to see that beautiful smile every time we lock eyes. But like I said before I wasn't good enough.

Love is a beautiful thing, but too bad I can't experience it, why? Because what I notice is that I get treated differently from the other guys. Most guys receive treatment that I feel like I deserve or things I may appreciate more then the current guy in her life. From a female's perspective they would consider me "soft" because I care about them. I wish I could just dive in her mind so I could swim through her thoughts to see what I can find, but she refuses to get close to me for what reason you ask? I still haven't quite figured it out. Older ladies that ask do I have someone special in my life I tell them the same story that I'm telling the readers. They always say, "If I Was Them Girls, I Would of Broke My Neck to Talk to You", but I guess every female doesn't think the same. Without that special girl my life feels pointless, who am I going to love? Who going to love me for me? I always seem to be the problem in almost every situation, they always ready to leave me. There is no better feeling in the world but to come home after a long horrible day to a beautiful woman ready to massage your shoulders & also ready to hear about your day. I guess "Yahweh" doesn't have anyone planned for me in the future, before I started feeling this way there was a girl name Nire.

Leu was special to me, but Nire had my heart in her hands. I met Nire on social media, she was so beautiful with her pretty brown skin along with her four eyes. Ha-ha that always makes me laugh every time I say it, but her mind is aesthetic & she has a good head on her shoulders. Her GPA is higher than mine & I have an extremely high GPA. It felt good to finally find someone who accepts me for me & not nobody that just want me for what I can do for them. Overtime we begin to love each other more & more every day, but of course at times there were issues. Do you enjoy being ugly? I do because if she says "I love you" I know that she truly means it. Honestly, I don't think she truly understands how she makes me feel. It's times when we talked on the phone & I started wondering what she may be thinking about whenever she stares at me. She would say "nothing, I'm not thinking about anything", but I would never continue the conversation because sooner or later it would spark an argument. I believe she is the love of my life, but I don't think she takes my words seriously sometimes. Actions speak louder than words, but lately I haven't had a chance to show her. I don't think she feels the same way about me, but I just can't live without her. A couple days would go by & I would start going crazy if I don't get a text or phone call from her.

I never wanted to be with someone so bad in my life, it's a feeling that I never felt before. I feel like every dude is wasting her time, it's times when I want to have a heart to heart conversation with Nire to see if we both are on the same page, but I always pick the wrong time. One day I thought about buying her a promise ring to show her how much I appreciate her. When I'm in her presence I can be myself without being judged, she gives me this certain vibe that is unexplainable. I learned overtime that even though we are not together, I am truly blessed that she is still in my life. I rather have her in my life as a friend then to not have her in my life at all. It's amazing how another human being can make your day 10 times better just by simply texting you. I wonder if I'm on her mind? I wonder do she still have feelings for me? When she says she loves me is it a friend love? Or is it a more special type of love? When her name pops up on my screen, I instantly crack a smile, I could be having a terrible day & there goes Nire coming to the rescue. She keeps me sane whenever I'm out of my freaking mind. I almost shed a tear just thinking about the past, I'm hoping we can start over I pray that break up was our last. If your reading this I hope you feel the same, I've been wanting to tell you this for so long, but I was afraid so I guess I'll take the blame. Man, it feels good to get that off my chest, my mind has been filled with thoughts, theories, & air pockets for months. I feel like I just had my own little "Therapy Session", but this only a temporary relief sort of like the teenage boy in the bathroom shooting Heroin. I think I found my coping mechanism for when the stress starts to become overwhelming. I think the feelings I had for Leu were more so artificial than real because I know I wasn't the only guy who had feelings for her. There were several more on the list, but she just never mentioned their names around me. Come to find out I was number 2 out of 10 boys who were attracted to her, so I just separated myself from that situation. Nire on the other hand is more than real because we understand each other more & we both know how to deal with each other. I may have to purchase a journal & keep it locked up in a safe place because there is still more that I have to say. The feeling of telling secrets without them being exposed to the world makes me feel good inside. It's like I can be myself whenever I write because nobody is there to judge me. I've talked myself to death, maybe I should try getting some sleep. I'm sitting up all night long like I don't have school in the morning. I tried falling asleep, but the feeling of self-destruction crossed my mind from the trauma that I had experienced 11th grade year. It was another devastating event that occurred when I was only 16 years old, by a careless individual named Isabella Copeland.

4

Sentimental

March 30th, 2017 I was heading over Isabella's house & at the time she was my girlfriend. I texted her & gave her a heads up letting her know I was on my way to her house, & that I will be there in 10 mins. She replies, "ok, oh & by the way my cousin is over here is that cool"? I replied yes, no problem. 10 mins went by I was now approaching the house, I felt this intense pain in my stomach, it was a feeling that I don't usually have every day only when I feel something isn't right. My thoughts were racing, it felt like my brain was the NASCAR track & my neurons & nerve impulses were the racers racing on the track. One side of my brain was telling me to just knock on the door & the other side was telling me to walk to the window & peak in. I thought about the saying "Looking from the outside in" maybe I was just assuming something maybe going on inside the house. But at the same time, I don't know what could be going on between them or the story that led up to their performance. I completely cleared my mind & approached the window slowly, I felt like I had mastered the stealth skill at that point. When I peeked through the window, I seen her "cousin" hands wrapped around her waist & then he started to feel down her left buttock.

I moved a little closer to the window & they started kissing, but it wasn't just an ordinary kiss. They both were swapping each other's saliva back & forth, it was such a heart-breaking sight. "Hey!! what the hell are you doing"? I said. "oh my gosh babe it's not what you think" Isabella said. "what the hell do you mean it's not what I think what else could it be? I thought this guy was your cousin?" I said. I completely snapped & before you know it, I was punching her living room window. When I broke the glass, I climbed into her window to have a little talk with her "cousin". Without even thinking I punched the guy in his jaw & saliva went flying in the air during the process of him falling to the floor. "Noremac stop!!! you're hurting him!!!" Isabella said. "Wow! so now you care about this kid huh"? my body started to shut down & I started to loosen my grip on his shirt, "I knew you didn't care about me, we never could have a decent conversation without your phone being in your hand, and it was all because he was in the picture now the puzzle is finally piecing all together" I said. "sorry Noremac I just don't like you anymore" Isabella said, "You don't like me anymore? I thought you loved me"? I said. "No, I never loved you Noremac all the love & affection that I was supposed to give to you I was giving it all to him" Isabella said. My heart started working overtime & my body started getting super-hot, but all I could remember is falling to the floor laying in my own puddle of tears.

"I knew you would react this way Noremac" Isabella said. Then why would you hurt me like this? "come with me on the porch so we can talk", what can we possibly talk about!!? "I'm really sorry I hurt your feelings, but you just not my type, I need someone who is cocky & more of a bad boy then a regular kid who sits in the house & write in his journal all day drowning in his own thoughts". I was silent I didn't know what to say or what to think, I was in complete shock. "But we can still be friends" Isabella said. "No, I don't think I even want to be your associate I hope your happy now" I said. I jumped off the porch with depression written all over my face & I started running down the street like a thirteen-year-old kid who is upset with his family members. "Noremac come back"!! Isabella said. I ignored her & kept running, I made it to an empty road it was so quiet all you can hear is the crickets rubbing their leathery wings together. Now since I'm alone I can finally process everything that just happened. I thought to myself what is trust? Is it something I should have? How hard is it to trust someone? I didn't know if I should continue to love her & suffer while being in the friend zone? Or should I say forget everything & just start cheating on every girl that I come across? I didn't know what to do.

Wait a second, I can't hurt every female that I come across that's just not me. I'm not like those other guys so why would I change now just because I had a little break up. If I had that mentality, I would never find the girl of my dreams. My problem is that I fall in love too easily, I could see a beautiful girl that's intelligent with a goofy personality, I would instantly fall to my knees & praise her as if she was a queen. But I just seem to do that to the wrong females, the girls I should be kneeling for I never do because my interest level is too low. I refuse to go down this route again I will not follow in the footsteps of Isabella & I will be the bigger person in this tragic situation. All there is left to do is go home & take a nap, maybe I can clear my mind & forget about it when I wake up. Wow just from reminiscing about this horrible day made my eyes swell up like I'm having an anaphylactic reaction. I can't keep holding onto the past because eventually it will determine my future. I will become miserable & bitter when it comes to women & at the end of the day, I will only be hurting myself. Nire if your reading this just know that I want you to be in my life forever regardless if we are a couple or not. I was afraid to tell you how I felt in reality, so I tried explaining myself to you indirectly.

5

Manipulation

Social media has a strong grip on adolescents nowadays, especially in this generation. Teens tend to follow trends & people that have the most fame, so you could consider most teens as followers. Instead of being a kid going outside & having fun with your friends, they just sit home & be on social media all day. Technology is the invention that caused a lot of people to become less active & lazy. Don't get me wrong technology is very helpful but can also hurt you in the process. If you were to interview a kid asking them what do they do on their spare time? Most would say watch tv or lay around yes, they would do that but at the same time they will be on their phones as well. Smart phones are the best way to manipulate a kid because in their mind they must have their smart phone, or they wouldn't be able to function properly. Also, on social media there is a lot of drama & chaos that teens love to fall into which takes their minds off what's really important. For example: two rappers are arguing on social media all the kids are so wrapped up in the argument, so they missed when the president bombed a foreign country for no apparent reason & there is a high chance, we are about to have a world war 3. Simple things can easily control someone's mind, such as video games, cell phones, computers & other types of technology. Should I let technology take over me? or should I fight it? I have yet to decide my final decision.

Not only does it manipulate you, but it also can cause you to become addicted to it. It will become a day to day routine for you, to wake up & check your phone for any messages or missed phone calls. Along with the "Video Games" which is my addiction, but I consider it more of a coping mechanism because it takes my mind off things for a short period of time & then boom the stress is in my presence again. I know a lot of closed-minded people who gets manipulated on the daily & they don't even notice it. Even though slavery ended several years ago we are technically still slaves. We are "Mentally Enslaved" because we can't live without materialistic things. We use materials to add wealth to ourselves & that is a big part of manipulation. Most people don't think much of themselves or they may think that they are a nobody, until they buy the newest pair of Air Jordan's, that everyone else has or a Louis Vuitton Bag, or a foreign car, then they would feel like a somebody. They use wealth to replace their self-worth & that is what society wants, they want everybody to spend money on expensive clothing & jewelry instead of spending money on things that's more important. Like saving for your own house or investing in a business it doesn't hurt to spend money on things you like or want, but at the same time buy things that's reasonable & not things that will break your pockets.

I was in school the other day & I seen a large crowd of kids surrounding a senior & they all were looking at his cellphone. My brothers wanted to know what was going on & so did I, so we walked in the middle of the large crowd & we seen on the senior cell phone these two girls fighting. The fight was popular because it was all over the internet & every kid in every school was talking about it. I immediately turned away & left the crowd, seeing things like that contaminates the human brain & it is hard to decontaminate it out of your system. In other words, once you see something negative, which is exciting to teenagers you will never forget what happen & you will eventually start to make up lies about someone to help start another fight, which is what everyone call instigating. What the kids failed to acknowledge is that the ice caps in Antarctica is melting due to global warming & eventually at any moment the world can become flooded & millions of people can possibly be killed, but teenagers don't care. Most teens are living in the moment, instead of thinking about tomorrow, next week, or even next year. It's good to think ahead so you can gather a plan to prepare for whatever may happen. I tried caressing teens with my words, but they consider me irrelevant because I refuse to drink & smoke the rest of my adolescent years away.

Teens need to learn to balance things out in life, because too much of anything is not a good thing. Certain hours of the day you can enjoy your electronics, then go outside & have fun for a couple hours. Do you ever notice when you go to parties or family gatherings people are always on their cell phones? Most people can't even engage in a conversation without checking their social media notifications. That lets you know that people can't live without technology. Before I was born family, time was crucial while the little kids playing around all the grown folks would drink & play cards. That's when gatherings were fun & exciting, but now it's all about the phone screen. I have a message to the soon to be mother's & father's you should try keeping your children active & away from the tv screen as much as possible. Most people don't believe in opening their minds to new things or opening their eyes to things they never paid attention to before. The reason is because society doesn't want you to be aware of things that's going on around you, they only want you to focus on the drama that's on tv & the celebrity lives. Ever met a gorgeous female or a very attractive guy, but they always put social media before you? you wonder why?

Because they are brainwashed. All they know is social media, drama, & taking pictures with filters. The people that are fully aware of everything that's going on around them or the people who don't take any bullshit are considered "woke" & are one of the most hated people in the world... STAY WOKE!

6

Drowning

Your adolescent years are the years that you need to enjoy, because you will never get them back, but at the same time don't do anything stupid that will cause permanent damage to your vital organs. High school kids love to party, get high, & get drunk. I have yet to see the hype in getting high or drunk every single day. It's times when you want to just chill & be alone in your room, but maybe that's just me. Most of the girls at my school are alcoholics & will drink anything you hand to them. The boys would only drink because there is a 50/50 chance, they can get in one of the girls' pants since they are intoxicated. As soon as a pretty girl finishes her drink, the boys bum rush each other to give her another bottle or shot. Parties is just not for me I just rather be alone or either be with my brothers. Some people don't even want to socialize with you if you don't drink or smoke & I find it odd, because you rather be around people who are using you for what you can provide for them, instead of looking for real true friends. After a while the people that are using you will eventually cut you off & then you will start to feel stupid & eventually start searching for real friends & they will be nowhere to be found.

Just from the thought turns my stomach, the odor of 5 different alcohol beverages on someone's breath. Now I have to go home & wash my brain, so I can forget about the image I just pictured. I'm so tired of going to school every day, its draining all my ATP out of my body. I walked into school this morning feeling relieved thank god it's Friday. As I was walking to first period some of my classmates were handing out invitations for today's party at Elizabeth's house. Elizabeth is one of the most popular girls in the entire school & to conversate with her you must have more than 10 tattoos, All F's on your report card, & you must wear only designer clothes. I didn't stand a chance, when I turned the corner Nedaj, Novad, & Nomad ran to me. "Bro we have to go to this party tonight" they said. Sorry dudes I don't do parties & you guys know this. "Yes, we know you don't like parties, but still bro come on just this one party" my brothers said. Why do you want to go to this girl party so damn bad? I said. "Because we want some action, we go there get a couple babes wasted take them to an empty room & have a good time". I like the sound of that I said. "we all do so are you in?". Sure, why not, I said in a not so interested tone. "Yes! let's meet at Nomad's house at 8:00 p.m."

Peer pressure at it's finest, they always convince me to do something I really don't want to do, but I only do it because I want to be cool like every other boy in school. It was now 8:00 p.m. I was standing outside of Nomad's house with Novad & Nedaj we knocked several times & didn't get an answer. So, something told me to look through his living room window & there he was on the couch half sleep with a spliff in his hand. "Ha-ha look at him he just couldn't help himself, why did he get high so early?" Novad said. We were laughing so loudly outside of his window that he jumped up out of his sleep & fell off the couch. When he started to get up his pupils locked onto the window & he noticed it was us & he begin to laugh with us. "Are you finish making a fool out of yourself?" Nedaj said. "Ha-ha very funny come on let's go to this damn party before I change my mind" Nomad said. Oh, hell no you dragged me out of the house you better go to this party, I said. Nomad got dressed & we were now on our way to Elizabeth's house. When we arrived at Elizabeth's party people were already wasted, there were guys throwing glass bottles in the middle of the street & guys were vomiting on the pavement while waiting on their ride to arrive. The party was a disaster already & we didn't even step foot in the house yet.

When we walked into the house, I was the only one looking suspicious & feeling skeptical. I told myself continuously what am I doing here? I should of never came here in the first place. Why did I let my friends persuade me into coming here? "Well if you'll excuse me, I'm about to grab a drink & talk to some babes", Nedaj said. I'm going to go sit in the corner while everyone else have fun deuces. "Now why would you do that?", Nomad & Novad said. Umm because I hate parties & I can't fit into environments like this. "Just try you'll be fine" Novad said. I ignored him & went to go find a comfortable spot in the corner, because I plan on being in that spot the entire time. Watching everyone stumble & fall over made me feel even more antisocial. I'm sitting in the corner under clouds of cannabis & this girl is yelling over the music making it hard to hear. I'm sitting next to a boy who's regurgitating I guess he been drinking way too much, oh my god why the hell am I here? I said to myself. The crowd singing songs that I never heard of, I just need to tell my friends that I will wait for them outside of Elizabeth's house until the party is over. I don't understand why do teenagers want to drink & smoke their life away? I thought you supposed to face the bottle or the spliff only if your stressed out, but apparently, I was wrong.

Three hours into the party, several drunk females are walking up to me asking me did I want a drink. I continued to tell them no until I finally came to my senses & decided I should have fun for once. I was called crazy before because I don't have interest in drinking or smoking am I crazy? Or are those people that asked that question incompetent? I have yet to crack that difficult code. I took my first sip & my face instantly frowned like I smelled something that was malodorous. "HA-HA YOU NEED TO MIX IT WITH CRANBERRY JUICE!!" the intoxicated girl said yelling over the deafening music. I took her advice & mixed the drink with cranberry juice & it was scrumptious. What is this? I asked, "Grey Goose" the intoxicated girl said. I took 5 more gulps & begin to feel woozy, where are my brothers? I need to talk to them. "LET THEM HAVE FUN JUST ENJOY YOUR DRINK!!". I was quite surprised I listened to her because usually I'm very stubborn when it comes to making decisions. "WHAT'S YOUR NAME"!? the intoxicated girl said, MY NAME IS NOREMAC!. WHAT'S YOUR NAME!? "CINDY!" NICE TO MEET YOU I said. I LOVE HOW THIS MAKES ME FEEL I WANT ANOTHER ROUND!!, "ALRIGHT! I'M IMPRESSED I THOUGHT YOU WOULD HAVE BEEN READY TO PUKE BY NOW" Cindy said. Cindy came back with round 2 of Grey Goose & after the 3rd gulp I fell to the floor & all I could hear is people screaming "help someone just passed out".

When I passed out, I felt an intense pain sort of like the pain a child would feel when he is being taken away from his mother. It's like I went into this unconscious state & I became paralyzed from my neck down to my ankles. I felt my soul leaving my shell & there I knew I overdosed on alcohol. Even though it was only 2 medium sized cups of Grey Goose, my system couldn't seem to handle the poison. When I opened my eyes all I seen was a white void & nothing was around & my friends were nowhere to be found. Hello!! Where am I? please don't say I'm dead please! I heard a voice in the distance, "Your half dead my child, but not completely yet". I looked around the vicinity & I seen no one around me, who could be speaking to me? I said to myself. Before I could respond to the mysterious voice, I woke back up & the entire house were surrounding me along with my brothers who were drunk. "Bro are you okay" I didn't respond I was too busy trying to figure how my soul just fell back into my body the way it did. I looked at my body & I was completely soaked with water, I never thought water could resurrect someone. I will never in my life drink again especially at a house party. I look at alcohol now as a suicide attempt because the poison is killing you slowly every time you drink it. I got up off the floor & immediately left the party with terror & anxiety. In the back of my mind I still wonder why people want to drink their lives away.

7

Posession

Did you ever like someone & they like you also, but will not make things happen because their friend is in their ear? Feeding them lies about you & telling them things you never did before. I consider those people possessed because someone else is in control of them. They can't seem to think on their own, so they run to a friend & ask should or should they not get in a relationship with you. You should never live through someone it's like your living their life & you are stopping them from living their own life. Overtime my mentality started to change because I noticed every time, I try to get close to a girl I always end up getting hurt. Maybe it's not my time to be in love, I get turned down every way you could think of. She either tells me she doesn't have interest in me herself, her friend would tell me she doesn't have interest in me even though it's a lie, but she just doesn't want her friend talking to me, or her friend dislikes me & then the girl looks at me differently, all because of what her friend thinks. After a while I begin to self-destruct because no matter where I go someone I want will always turn me down & someone I never even acknowledged before will stand in front of me & tell me how much they want me & they be the ones that I need in my life. I find it ironic that the ones you want will put a hand in your face & the ones who are attracted to you, you end up repeating what your crush did to you.

An imbecile once told me "You must reach my friends expectations in order for me to talk to you". This quote pulled me back to manipulation, therefore she's nothing without her master. Her mind is sealed like a bank vault there is no way you can open it without the combination. This is what I like to call "out of sight, out of mind" meaning if I never acknowledge you, I would never think about you. That saves me from stressing myself out over a rejection that could have been avoided. If you were in my situation would you continue to break your heart to pieces trying to make something happen that you know will never happen? Or would you just let the girl go? Some people tend to stay in their friend's business when it comes to their relationships. "How's your relationship going?" or What do you guys do when your alone?" Information no member of the relationship should answer. The reason for this is because their lonely so they want to live through their friends to kind of make them feel less lonely as possible. I could never live through a friend because I would want to do things differently from what they do. I'm content with spending all my time by myself, but after a while it does get lonely.

Sometimes the media & the people will make you feel weird or out of place if you're not in a relationship but being single is actually rewarding. Being single shows you that you can be independent. For some of us maybe we don't have other halves. Maybe some of us are whole, and our only soulmates are ourselves. I never thought of it that way until now. How come it's so hard to find someone with the same mindset as me, or at least a similar mindset. It gives me a migraine just thinking about all the bad luck I've been having lately. To be honest the readers are living vicariously through me right now. The audience is walking through the shoes of Noremac trying to help me find myself. Also, parents can live vicariously through their children, by choosing a path for them instead of letting them choose a path on their own. Some parents want their children to finish their legacy, but it never go as planned. My high school teacher told me "You're going to college I don't care how you feel about it" & I was offended because I don't have a father in my life so what makes you think I'm going to listen to him. I had to find my own passion & follow my own dream in order to make myself happy. But along the way there are many trials & tribulations you will encounter before you get to the end of the road.

8

T.T.O.P

Trials & tribulations is something you will encounter when trying to accomplish a goal, but having enough passion allows you to conquer your dreams. What's your passion? I think my calling is writing I may grow up & become an author or a journalist one day. Maybe I might find interest in creating things, so I may become an inventor, or I might find interest in music & become a music producer. Ever since I wrote in my journal, I started to feel better & more at ease with myself because I can release all my emotions just by talking about what I did today. But there were several things that stopped me from becoming a writer. The sky isn't the limit, but the only thing that's truly stopping you from living your dream is yourself. That was my problem I always worried about what people thought of me & what were the people going to say when I tell them I want to become a writer. Haters was another group of people who stopped me from becoming a writer because they always tell me "you're not going to make it" & "you suck at writing I don't know why you even trying". It used to get to me, but after a while I blocked the negativity out & just kept telling myself "As long as I believe in myself that's all that matters". The last thing that stopped me from becoming a writer were females.

Females are the biggest distractions that you can have in your life as a teenager. Females was a distraction for me because I couldn't focus on writing & trying to get a girlfriend at the same time it was either one or the other. I had to give one of them my full attention, but it was a hard choice to make. I overheard a conversation while passing through the hallway of a couple arguing over something that was stupid. "Babe can you come over my house afterschool I have the place all to myself?" the girl said. "No, I'm sorry I have to stay after school to finish my project" the boy said. "Oh, come on please for me?" the girl said "I'm afraid not babe I will see you later tonight" the boy said. "Ugh okay!" the girl said while frowning her face & folding her arms. "Fine"! If I was in this situation I would of chose school over her as well because one of us has to have a good education even though we both need it. She thinks just because her parents aren't home, he should automatically cancel his plans & come over her house. No, you should always choose school over punani because once they wrap you around their finger you can kiss your good grades goodbye. Some females think the world only revolves around them, but it doesn't & you have to let her know that & if she can't seem to understand that then she isn't the right girl for you.

In high school a friend of mine wrote a novel called "Apicology" meaning the study of heartbreak. It was about things that the author couldn't quite get through people minds verbally so he had to write it in third person to tell his story in a secretive way. He mentions being homeless, & the suicidal thoughts that ran through his mind while riding in the passenger seat trying to find a decent dark place to sleep. His trials & tribulations were surviving on the street until they were able to get into a home again. Ever since I read his novel my life changed for the better, I started appreciating things that I always took for granted. I always took my life for granted by doing dangerous things & I never thanked Yahweh for waking me up every morning & allowing me to dodge death every time I face it. I wonder what death is like? Is it a better place than the world we're living in? Do the people that die ever come back? Will my soul haunt the living? I'm surprised I lasted this long in life because it is difficult living without a father, I wish he had loved me enough to stay in my life, but I guess I didn't matter to him. I guess I didn't mean shit to him, maybe I will never be shit. He treated my other siblings better than me, I wouldn't be surprised if he really didn't want me.

9

Narcissistic

People pay attention to the wrong things while the teens asking their friends should they throw a party, they should be filling out applications to provide for their family. They rather pay for attention instead of paying attention to the people who is only in their life for certain reasons. Grown folks paying $50,000 for a watch just to see what time the uber coming. The teenage boys paying $250 or more for a belt that no one will ever see because their shirt covers it. Some people wonder why they always broke because they always trying to look rich by living beyond their means. If they saved every dollar, they spent at the jewelry store they should have had their own house by now. If they saved every dollar, they spent on getting a uber they should have had their own car by now. You have to stop living in the moment you have to make a scheme, because the system is made for us to fail, you just have to show them you're not a product of your environment. Just imagine you on a date with a beautiful girl at a fancy restaurant when you should be home spending time with your kids. The waiter gives you the check the total is out of your budget, so you have to spend the money you had saved for your kids Christmas presents. To make it seem like you have money like that, if you knew the bill was going to be high you should of went to the nearest food spot & bought both of you a reasonable price meal.

You should motivate yourself to live a life to impress parents, instead of striving to live a life to impress your social media & temporary friends. Now all your money gone what are you going to tell your kids? "Daddy got robbed for his money" until your baby mother pulls your card. Her friend was at the same restaurant as you, scoping the place out & then she came across you. Then she picked up the phone & started dialing your children's mother, now the hole you fell into is getting deeper & harder to climb out of. While you in the club spending $300 on a bottle that you know is worth $15 & your family is at home in the kitchen looking through empty cabinets. Your priorities are messed up, & you claim that your living life, but at least spend your money more wisely & on the things that matter. Instead of showing off with $800 shoes, why not buy a pair of shoes that's reasonable & more of in your budget. Stop trying to live the life of a superstar when at the end of the day you go home to a raggedy apartment. If you want to live beyond your means at least have a car & a house to match what you are wearing. Don't have an old busted up car, with an apartment in a poor neighborhood. But you wearing a Burberry shirt, with a Louis Vuitton Belt, with some Balmain Jeans & some Gucci Shoes. Then when he run out of money, he wants to face the bottle or roll a spliff to help forget about his problems, when you were the one from the jump that put yourself in this situation.

While your young you should make & save your money, so when it comes time to retire you can go on vacation with your family & live life. But people choose to live it up now & worry about today, instead of worrying about their future. You will never see too many people think like me, because everybody wants what everybody already has. Why you think they build liquor stores in poor neighborhoods? for guys like you that don't make the most but you spend the most. People continue to try to look rich on a broke income or no income at all, just to impress people that don't give a shit about you. I refuse to expire in poverty; my wife & my seeds are going to live the best life because I will sacrifice anything just to see them happy. I learned to feed my mind with knowledge & not my ego because anything that's easy to get isn't worth getting & anything that's difficult is worth fighting for. A person without common knowledge wouldn't know any better, all they would know is men, woman, smoking spliffs, & popping bottles. This generation is slowly deteriorating, because there aren't enough fathers to teach their son's how to be men & there aren't enough mother's teaching their daughter's how to be intelligent young women.

10

Deadbeat

When my father left the picture, my heart became cold & for years I didn't care about anything. Someone could be getting jumped & I would just walk right past them like nothing happened. He left when I was 7 years old & I was too young to understand why. Last time he came to see me is when my bike chain popped. Not to mention the chain popped again & I called him to ask can he teach me how to fix it on my own. Dad, my chain popped again can you come fix it whenever you get a chance I said. "Yeah I will stop pass on my lunch break". I was sitting outside waiting for his arrival with my broken bike. It was 4:30 PM & my curfew was at 6:00 PM so I didn't have to much longer to stay outside. The clock struck 6:00 PM & my father was nowhere to be found, there was no phone call letting me know why he didn't come or nothing. The way I talk about my father people think he passed away, but he's still alive he's just dead to me. Where was he when I first hit puberty? Where was he when I was leaving for prom? Where was he when I walked across the stage? I'm trying to hold my tears back, but it's not working so well. How could you do this shit to me? What the hell were you thinking? How can you just abandon your kids the way you did & still live life like everything is okay?

Are you fucking happy? did you get what you wanted? It's not like you cared for me anyway, you missed my birthday eleven times how could I ever forgive you. I have to call you first just to talk to my own father & when you answer you always say "hey!!" like you so surprised to hear from me. If you knew you wasn't going to be in my life, why would you have me. On my 13th birthday my mom asked my sperm donor could he come see me for a few minutes. "I can't I have to work". The words that he said knocked the air out of my lungs & my eyes begin to fill with tears. All my friend's fathers were in their lives & I was the only one who had only one parent. How can he live with himself knowing he will never talk to his son again? Does he even love me? Because a man that truly love his kids will do anything to talk to his kids. Fuck you I hope you grow old & none of your kids come & see you when you in the nursing home. I hope Yah make you suffer every way possible. How could you do this to me all I did was show nothing but love to you & you do this shit to me. I need a spliff or some more alcohol maybe this time I will pass out & don't wake up.

This situation hurt me so bad that I started looking for a father figure in my friend's fathers. One of my closest friend's father always gave me money when he seen me & asked me how I was doing in school. My friend used to always say "where is your father"? & I always told him he's at work even though I didn't have a clue where he was. It's a shame how he put his job before his own children. Maybe I was a burden to him & he just couldn't handle work & taking care of me all at the same time. I'm always a problem maybe the world would be a better place if I wasn't here. Girls use me for what I can do for them, I'm forced to grow up, so I have to learn everything on my own. I don't want to have kids because I don't know how to be a father. I refuse to repeat the same thing my father did to me. I don't know how to be a man, so I can't be in a relationship. Maybe I should die alone because no female in this world will ever love me for me. Maybe I should just end this tragedy before it gets worse. I hope your happy, I'm doing something you always wanted me to do ever since I was born. Don't even shed a tear for me because once you leave the room it's just going to dry up & a big smile will appear on your face. Go ahead & call me a coward & say that I'm not strong because I can't deal with the pain. You always said "you are your mother's child" maybe your right.

"A Letter TO You"

Dear Readers,

    Throughout my journey I've experienced several things from finding the group I feel most comfortable in, deciding whether or not I should do narcotics, falling in love with girls who never had interest in me, reminiscing about a break up that still crushes me, the powerful grip social media has on the youth, drinking my life away, living through your friends, the trials & tribulations you encounter when chasing your dream or passion, spending money on things that's not important, & last but not least growing up fatherless. From experiencing those things, I realized I don't want to deal with any of this anymore. No matter what group I choose I will always be hated, I will never get the love I deserve, I will never have friends because I don't drink or smoke, I will never catch my dream, & My father will never love me. I know there's consequences coming my way because of my actions, but that's just life. I shall end my nightmare while I still have a the chance.

Sincerely, Noremac

A week later... "Bro you mind dropping me off at Noremac's house I haven't heard from him in a week & he haven't been answering my calls or text messages" Nedaj said. Knock knock knock "yo Noremac I know you in there", "Are you sure he's in the house" Nomad & Novad said. "No shit all this man do is write & listen to music all day" Nedaj said. Nedaj twist the knob & came into the house "hello is anybody here!" there was no response. He walked up the steps yelling Noremac's name "Stop playing these games bro" when he reached the top of the steps, he seen Noremac's room door wide open. "Look bro I'm not playing these hide & seek games with you" Nedaj said. He walked in Noremac's room & spotted a note on his bed. Nomad & Novad ran up the stairs to help assist Nedaj on figuring out what had happened to Noremac. "Here's a letter" Nedaj said, "who is it for" Novad & Nomad said. "The Readers" Nedaj said. "Who are the readers" Novad said. "I don't know" Nedaj said. "Wait, do you guys here something it sounds like water running" Nomad said. The brothers went to the bathroom & opened the door & you would not believe what they saw. Noremac unconscious in his bathtub. The water was covering his entire body & it was so hot that it was difficult to check his carotid pulse to see if he was still alive. Noremac's skin began to peel away like he had some sort of skin disease. The water was so hot it was like putting your hands on a scalding hot stove. "No No No bro please wake up"! don't leave me here please"

Printed in the United States
By Bookmasters